ספר יצירה

SEPHER YETZIRAH

OR

THE BOOK OF FORMATION

AND THE

THIRTY TWO PATHS OF WISDOM

Translated from the Hebrew

by

WM. WYNN. WESCOTT. M.B

Supreme Magus of the Soc. Ros. in Anglia.

Copyright © 2015 A Mystical World Reprints
All rights reserved.
ISBN - 10: 1537459058
ISBN - 13: 978- 1537459059

Contents.

Preface to the Second Edition			01
Introduction			02
Chapter	I.	Sephiroth, Numbers, Letters	09
"	II.	The Twenty-Two Letters	11
"	III.	The Triad	12
"	IV.	The Heptad	13
"	"	Supplement	13
"	V.	The Dodecad	15
"	"	Supplement	15
"	VI.	Conclusion	17
The Thirty-Two Paths of Wisdom			19
Notes to the Sepher Yetzirah			23
Notes to the Thirty-Two Paths			32

PREFACE TO THE SECOND EDITION.

IT has been at the earnest wish of many students, members of the Theosophical Society, and of my Hermetic fratres of the Order of the G.D., that I have made a revised translation of the "Sepher Yetzirah." In this edition I have followed most closely the Hebrew version of Joannes Stephanus Rittangelius, which was printed in 1642 at Amsterdam, and I have forsaken many of the Latinised renderings which had been adopted in the First Edition, from the works of Postellus and Pistorius.

The Notes have been extended, and it is hoped that they explain and illustrate difficult passages, and render this abstruse treatise more comprehensible than it has been hitherto found.

W. W.W., F.T.S.

SEPHER YETZIRAH.

INTRODUCTION.

THE "Sepher Yetzirah," or "Book of Formation," is perhaps the oldest philosophical treatise which is yet extant in the Hebrew language. The great interest which has been evinced of late years in the Hebrew Kabalah, and the modes of thought and doctrine allied to it, has induced me to translate this volume from the original Hebrew texts, and to collate with them the Latin versions of mediaeval authorities. Three important books of the "Zohar," or "Splendour," which is the great storehouse of Kabalistic teaching, have been for the first time translated into English by that skilful and erudite Kabalist, my fellow student in occult science, MacGregor Mathers, and the "Sepher Yetzirah" in an English translation is almost a necessary companion to these even more abstruse disquisitions: the two books indeed mutually explain each other.

The "Sepher Yetzirah" although this name means "The Book of Formation," is not in any sense a narrative of Creation, or a substitute Genesis, but it is a very ancient and instructive philosophical treatise upon one aspect of the origin of the universe and mankind; an aspect at once archaic and essentially Hebrew. The grouping of the processes of origin into an arrangement, at once alphabetic and numeral, is one only to be found in Semitic authors.

Attention must be called to the essential peculiarity of Hebrew doctrines, the inextricable and necessary association of numbers and letters; every letter suggesting a number, and every group of letters having a numerical signification, as vital as its literal meaning.

The Kabalistic principles involved in the reversal of Hebrew letters, and their substitution by others, on definite schemes, should also be studied and borne in mind.

It is exactly on these principles that the "groundwork idea" of this disquisition rests; and these principles may be traced throughout the Kabalistic volumes which have succeeded it in point of time, and development, and which are now associated together in one volume and known as the "Zohar," or "Book of Splendour," a collection of treaties which is in the main concerned with the essential dignities of the God-head, and with the emanations which have sprung there from, with the doctrine of the Sephiruth, and the ideals of Macroprosopus and Microprosopus.

The "Sepher Yetzirah," on the other hand is mainly concerned with our universe and with the Microcosm. The opinions of Hebrew Kabalistic Rabbis and of two French mystics may be fitly introduced here.

The following interesting comment is from Rabbi Moses Botarel:—"It was Abraham our Father—blessed be he—who wrote this book to condemn the doctrine of the sages of his time, who were incredulous of the supreme dogma of the Unity. At least, this was the opinion of Rabbi Saadiah—blessed be he—as written in the first chapter of his book 'The Philosopher's Stone.' These are his words: The sages of Babylon attacked Abraham on account of his faith; for they were ail against him although themselves separable into three sects. The First thought that the Universe was subject to the control of two opposing forces, the one existing but to destroy the other, this is dualism; they held that there was nothing in common between the author of evil and the author of good. The Second sect admitted Three great Powers; two of them as in the first case, and a third Power whose function was to decide between the two others, a supreme arbitrator. The Third sect recognised no god beside the Sun, in which it recognised the sole principle of existence."

Rabbi Judah Ha Levi, in his critical description of this treatise, wrote: "The Sepher Yetzirah teaches us the existence of a Single Divine Power by showing us that in the bosom of variety and multiplicity, there is, a Unity and Harmony, and that such universal concord could only arise from the rule of a Supreme Unity."

Eliphas Lévi, the famous French Occultist, thus wrote of the "Sepher Yetzirah," in his "Histoire de la Magie," p. 54: "The Zohar is a Genesis of illumination, the Sepher Jezirah is a ladder formed of truths. Therein are explained the thirty-two absolute signs of sounds, numbers and letters: each letter reproduces a number, an idea and a form; so that mathematics are capable of application to ideas and to forms not less rigorously than to numbers, by exact proportion and perfect correspondence. By the science of the Sepher Jezirah the human spirit is fixed to truth, and in reason, and is able to take account of the possible development of intelligence by the evolutions of numbers. The Zohar represents absolute truth, and the Sepher Jezirah provides the means by which we may seize, appropriate and make use of it."

Upon another page Eliphas Lévi writes: "The Sepher Jezirah and the Apocalypse are the masterpieces of Occultism; they contain more wisdom than words; their expression is as figurative as poetry, and at the same time it is as exact as mathematics."

In the volume entitled "La Kabbale" by the eminent French scholar and Membre de L'Institut, Adolphe Franck, there is a chapter on the "Sepher Yetzirah." He writes as follows:—

"The Book of Formation contains, I will not say a system of physics, but of cosmology such as could be conceived at an age and in a country where the habit of explaining all phenomena by the immediate action of the First Cause, tended to check the spirit of observation, and where in consequence certain general and superficial relations perceived in the natural world passed for the science of Nature." . . . "Its form is simple and grave; there is nothing like a demonstration nor an argument; but it consists rather of a series of aphorisms, regularly grouped, and which have all the conciseness of the most ancient oracles."

In his analysis of the "Sepher Yetzirah," he adds:— "The Book of Formation, even if it be not very voluminous, and if it do not altogether raise us to very elevated regions of thought, yet offers us at least a composition which is very homogeneous and of a rare originality. The clouds which the imagination of commentators have gathered around it, will be dissipated, if we look for, in it, not mysteries of ineffable wisdom, but an attempt at a reasonable doctrine, made when reason arose, an effort to grasp the plan of the universe, and to secure the link which binds to one common principle, all the elements which are around us."

"The last word of this system is the substitution of the absolute divine Unity for every idea of Dualism, for that pagan philosophy which saw in matter an eternal substance whose laws were not in accord with Divine Will; and for the Biblical doctrine, which by its idea of Creation, postulates two things, the Universe and God, as two substances absolutely distinct one from the other."

"In fact, in the 'Sepher Yetzirah,' God considered as the Infinite and consequently the indefinable Being, extended throughout all things by his power and existence, is while above, yet not outside of numbers, sounds and letters, — the principles and general laws which we recognise."

"Every element has its source from a higher form, and all things have their common origin from the Word (Logos), the Holy Spirit. . . So God is at once, in the highest sense, both the matter and the form of the universe. Yet He is not *only* that form; for nothing can or does exist outside of Himself; His substance is the foundation of all, and all things bear His imprint and are symbols of His intelligence."

Hebrew tradition assigns the doctrines of the oldest portions of the "Zohar" to a date antecedent to the building of the Second Temple, but Rabbi Simeon ben Jochai, who lived in the reign of the Emperor Titus, A.D. 70-80, is considered to have been the first to commit these to writing, and Rabbi Moses de Leon, of Gaudalaxara, in Spain, who died in 1305, certainly reproduced and published the "Zohar."

Ginsburg, speaking of the Zoharic doctrines of the Ain Suph, says that they were unknown until the 13th century, but he does not deny the great antiquity of the Sepher Yetzirah, in which it will be noticed the "Ain Suph Aur" and "Ain Suph" are not mentioned.

I suggest, however, that this omission is no proof that the doctrines of "Ain Suph Aur" and "Ain Suph" did not then exist, because it is a reasonable supposition, that the "Sepher Yetzirah" was the volume assigned to the Yetziratic World, the third of the four Kabalistic Worlds of Emanation, while the "Asch Metzareph" is concerned with the Assiatic, fourth, or lowest World of Shells, and is on the face of it an alchemical treatise; and again the "Siphra Dtzenioutha" may be fittingly considered to be an Aziluthic work, treating of the Emanations of Deity alone; and there was doubtless a fourth work assigned to the World of Briah—the second type, but I have not been able to identify this treatise.

Both the Babylonian and the Jerusalem Talmuds refer to the "Sepher Yetzirah." Their treatise named "Sanhedrin," certainly mentions the "Book of Formation," and another similar work; and Rashi in his commentary on the treatise "Erubin," considers this a reliable historical notice. This work then, or a similar predecessor, is at least as old as A.D. 200.

Other positive historical notices are those of Saadjah Gaon, who died A.D. 940, and Judah Halevi, A.D. 1150; both these Hebrew classics speak of it as a very ancient work.

The most generally accepted modern opinion is that the author was Rabbi Akiba, who lived in the time of the Emperor Hadrian, A.D. 120.

Graetz, however, assigns it to early Gnostic times, third or fourth century, and Zunz speaks of it as post Talmudical, and belonging to the Geonic period 700 to 800 A.D.; Rubinsohn, in the "Bibliotheca Sacra," speaks of this latter idea as having no real basis.

The Talmuds were first collected into a concrete whole, and printed in Venice, 1520 A.D.

The "Zohar" was first printed in Mantua in 1558, again in Cremona, 1560, and at Lublin, 1623, and a fourth edition by Knorr von Rosenroth, at Sulzbach in 1684. Some parts are not very ancient, since some versions mention the Crusades.

Six extant Hebrew editions of the "Sepher Yetzirah" were collected and printed at Lemberg in 1680. The oldest of these six recensions was that of Saadjah Gaon.

Commentaries by Judah Halevi, and by Eben Ezra, of the 12th century, are also known.

There are now to be found in the best libraries, several Latin versions, *viz.*, that of Gulielmus Postellus, 1552, Paris; one by Johann Pistorius, in his "Artis Cabalisticse Tomus," 1587, Basle; and a third by Joannes Stephanus Rittangelius, 1642, Amsterdam; this latter gives both Hebrew and Latin, and also the Thirty-Two Paths as a supplement.

There is also a good German translation, by Johann Friedrich von Meyer, dated 1830. Quite recently, and since the completion of my translation, my attention has been drawn to a version by Isidor Kalisch, in which he has reproduced many of the valuable annotations of Meyer. The edition which I now offer is fundamentally that of the ancient Hebrew codices translated into English, and collated with the Latin versions of Pistorius, Postellus, and Rittangelius. The following copies of the "Sepher Yetzirah" in Hebrew, I have also examined:—

1. A Version by Saadiah, abi ben David, and three others, Mantua, 1562, 4to.
2. A Version with the commentary of Rabbi Abraham F. Dior, Amsterdam, 1642, 4to.
3. A A Version with preface by M. ben J. Chagiz, Amsterdam, 1713, 16mo.

4.	A	Version,	Constantinople, 17 19, 8vo.
5.	"	"	Zolkiew, 1745, 4to.
6.	"	"	by Moses ben Jacob, Zozec, 1779, 4to.
7.	"	"	Grodno, 1806, 4to.
8.	"	"	Dyhernfurth, 1812, 8vo.
9.	"	"	Salonica, 1831, 8vo.
10.			A MSS. copy dated 1719, in the British Museum.

I add here the full titles of the three Latin versions; they are all to be found in the British Museum Library.

"Abrahami Patriarchæ Liber Jezirah sive Formationis Mundi, Patribus quidem Abrahami tempora præcedentibus revelatus, sed ab ipso etiam Abrahamo expositus Isaaco, et per prophetarum manus posteritati conservatus, ipsis autem 72. Moses auditoribus in secundo divinæ veritatis loco, hoc est in ratione quœ est posterior authoritate, habitus." Parisiis, 1552. Gulielmus Postellus.

"Id est Liber Jezirah, qui Abrahamos, Patriarchæ adscribitur, unacum Commentario Rabi Abraham F. D. super 32 semitis Sapientiæ, a quibus Liber Jezirah incipit: Translatus et notis illustratus a Joanne Stephano Rittangelio Ling. Orient, in Elect. Acad. Regiomontana Prof. Extraord," Amstelodami, 1642.

In Tomus Primus of "Artis Cabalisticæ hoc est reconditæ theologiæ et philosophiæ script orum." Basileæ 1587, is found "Liber de Creatione Cabalistinis, Hebraice Sepher Jezira; Authore Abrahamo. Successive filiis ore traditus. Hinc jam rebus Israel inclinatis ne deficeret per sapientes Hierusalem arcanis et profundissimis sensibus literis commendatus." Johannes Pistorius.

The "Sepher Yetzirah" consists of six chapters, having 33 paragraphs distributed among them, in this manner, the first has 12, then follow 5, 5, 4, 3, and 4.

The oldest title has, as an addition, the words, "The Letters of our Father Abraham" or "ascribed to the patriarch Abraham", and it is spoken of as such, by-many mediæval authorities: but this origin is doubtless fabulous although perhaps not more improbable than the supposed authorship of the "Book of Enoch," mentioned by St. Jude, and rescued in modern times from the wilds of Ethiopia by the great traveller Bruce.

In essence the work was, doubtless, the crystallization of centuries of tradition by one writer, and it has been added to from time to time, by later authors, who have also revised it.

Some of the additions, which were rejected even by mediaeval students, I have not incorporated with the text at all, and I present in this volume only the undoubted kernel of this occult nut, upon which many great authorities, Hebrew, German, Jesuit and others have written long commentaries, and yet have failed to explain satisfactorily.

I find Kalisch speaking of these Commentaries says, "they contain nothing but a medley of arbitrary explanations, and sophistical distortions of scriptural verses, astrological notions, oriental superstitions, a metaphysical jargon, a poor knowledge of physics, and not a correct elucidation of this ancient book." Kalisch, however, was not an occultist; these commentaries are, however, so extensive as to demand years of study, and I feel no hesitation in confessing that my researches into them have been but superficial.

For convenience of study I have placed the Notes in a separate form at the end of the work, and I have made a short definition of the subject-matter of each chapter.

The substance of this little volume was read as a Lecture before the Hermetic Society of London in the summer of 1886, Dr. Anna Kingsford, President, in the chair. Some of the Notes were the explanations given verbally, and subsequently in writing, to members of the Society who asked for information upon abstruse points in the "Sepher," and for collateral doctrines; others, of later date, are answers which have been given to enquiring Theosophists, and members of the Hermetic G. D.

The late Madame Blavatsky, my esteemed teacher of Theosophy, and my personal friend, at whose suggestion a friendly alliance between the Hermetic Order of the G. D. and the Inner Group of Theosophic students was made, expressed to me her recognition of the value of the "Sepher Yetzirah" as a mystical treatise on cosmic origin, and her approval of my work in its translation, and of my notes and explanations.

CHAPTER 1

SECTION I. In thirty-two[1] wonderful Paths of Wisdom did Jah[2], Jehovah Tzabaoth[3] the God of Israel[4], the Elohim of the living[5], the King of ages, the merciful and gracious God[6] the exalted One, the Dweller in eternity, most high and holy—engrave his name by the three Sepharim[7] — Numbers, Letters, and Sounds.[8]

2. Ten are the ineffable Sephiroth[9]. Twenty-two are the Letters, the Foundation of all things; there are Three Mothers, Seven Double and Twelve[10] Simple letters.

3. The ineffable Sephiroth are Ten, so are the Numbers; and as there are in man five fingers over against five, so over them is established a covenant of strength, by word of mouth, and by the circumcision of the flesh[11].

4. Ten is the number of the ineffable Sephiroth, ten and not nine, ten and not eleven. Understand this wisdom, and be wise in the perception. Search out concerning it, restore the Word to its creator, and replace Him who formed it upon his throne[12].

5. The Ten ineffable Sephiroth have ten vast regions bound unto them; boundless in origin and having no ending; an abyss[13] of good and of ill; measureless height and depth; boundless to the East and the West; boundless to the North and South[14]; and the Lord the only God[15], the Faithful King rules all these from his holyseat[16], for ever and ever.

6. The Ten ineffable Sephiroth have the appearance of the Lightning flash[17], their origin is unseen and no end is perceived. The Word is in them as they rush forth and as they return, they speak as from the whirlwind, and returning fall prostrate in adoration before the Throne.

7. The Ten ineffable Sephiroth, whose ending is even as their origin, are like as a flame arising from a burning coal. For God[18] is superlative in his Unity, there is none equal unto Him: what number canst thou place before One.

8. Ten are the ineffable Sephiroth; seal up thy lips lest thou speak of them, and guard thy heart as thou considerest them; and if thy mind escape from thee bring it back to thy control; even as it was said, "running and returning" (the living creatures ran and returned)[19] and hence was the Covenant made.

9. The ineffable Sephiroth give forth the Ten numbers. First; the Spirit of the God of the living[20]; Blessed and more than blessed be the Living God[21] of ages. The Voice, the Spirit, and the Word[22], these are of the Holy Spirit.

10. Second; from the Spirit He produced Air, and formed in it twenty-two sounds—the letters; three are mothers, seven are double, and twelve are simple; but the Spirit is first and above these. Third; from the Air He formed the Waters, and from the formless and void[23] made mire and clay, and designed surfaces upon them, and hewed recesses in them, and formed the strong material foundation. Fourth; from the Water He formed Fire[24] and made for Himself a Throne of Glory with Auphanim, Seraphim and Kerubim[25], as his ministering angels; and with these three[26] he completed his dwelling, as it is written, "Who maketh his angels spirits and his ministers a flaming fire".[27]

11. He selected three letters from among the simple ones and sealed them and formed them into a Great Name, IHV,[28] and with this He sealed the universe in six directions.

Fifth; He looked above, and sealed the Height with IHV.
Sixth; He looked below, and sealed the Depth with IVH.
Seventh; He looked forward, and sealed the East with HIV.
Eighth; He looked backward, and sealed the West with HVI.
Ninth; He looked to the right, and sealed the South with VIH.
Tenth; He looked to the left, and sealed the North with VHI.

12. Behold ! From the Ten ineffable Sephiroth do proceed — the One Spirit of the Gods of the living, Air, Water, Fire; and also Height, Depth, East, West, North and South.[29]

CHAPTER II

SECTION I. The twenty-two sounds and letters are the Foundation of all things. Three mothers, seven doubles and twelve simples. The Three Mothers are Aleph, Mem and Shin, they are Air, Water and Fire. Water is silent, Fire is sibilant, and Air derived from the Spirit is as the tongue of a balance standing between these contraries which are in equilibrium, reconciling and mediating between them.

2. He hath formed, weighed, and composed with these twenty-two letters every soul, and the soul of everything which shall hereafter be.

3. These twenty-two sounds or letters are formed by the voice, impressed on the air, and audibly modified in five places; in the throat, in the mouth, by the tongue, through the teeth, and by the lips[31].

4. These twenty-two letters, which are the foundation of all things, He arranged as upon a sphere with two hundred and thirty-one gates, and the sphere may be rotated forward or backward, whether for good or for evil: from the good comes true pleasure, from evil nought but torment.

5. For He showed the combination of these letters, each with the other; Aleph with all, and all with Aleph; Beth with all, and all with Beth. Thus in combining all together in pairs are produced the two hundred and thirty-one gates of knowledge[32].

6. And from the non-existent[33] He made Some-Thing; and all forms of speech and everything that has been produced; from the empty void He made the material world, and from, the inert earth He brought forth everything that hath life. He showed, as it were, vast columns out of the intangible air, and by the power of His Name made every creature and everything that is; and the production of all things from the twenty-two letters is the proof that they are all but parts of one body[34].

CHAPTER III

SECTION I. The Foundation of all others is composed of the Three Mothers, Aleph, Mem and Shin; they resemble a Balance, on the one hand the guilty, on the other hand the purified, and Aleph the Air is like the Tongue of a Balance standing between them.[35]

2. The Three Mothers Aleph, Mem and Shin are a great Mystery, very admirable and most recondite, and sealed as with six rings; and from them proceed Air, Fire, and Water, which divide into male and female forces. The Three Mothers Aleph, Mem and Shin are the Foundation, from them spring three Fathers, and from these have proceeded all things that are in the world.

3. The Three Mothers in the world are Aleph, Mem and Shin: the heavens[36] were produced[37] from Fire; the earth from the Water; and the Air from the Spirit is as a reconciler between the Fire and the Water.

4. The Three Mothers Aleph, Mem and Shin, Fire, Water and Air are shown in the Year; from the fire was made heat, from the waters was made cold, and from the air was produced the temperate state, again a mediator between them. The Three Mothers, Aleph, Mem and Shin, Fire, Water and Air are found in Man: from the fire was formed the head; from the water the belly; and from the air was formed the chest, again placed as a mediator between the others.

5. These Three Mothers did He produce and design, and combined them; and He sealed them as the three mothers in the Universe, in the Year and in Man — both male and female. He caused the letter Aleph to reign in Air and crowned it, and combining it with the others He sealed it, as Air in the World, as the temperate (climate) of the Year, and as the chest the lungs for breathing air) in Man: the male with A.M.S., the female with S.M.A. He caused the letter Mem to reign in Water, crowned it, and combining it with the others formed the earth in the world, cold in the year, and the belly in man, male and female, the former with M.A.S., the latter with M.S.A. He caused Shin to reign in Fire, and crowned it, and combining it with the others, sealed with it the heavens in the universe, heat in the year and the head in man, male and female[38].

CHAPTER IV

SECTION I. The Seven Double Letters, Beth, Gimel, Daleth, Kaph, Pé, Resh, and Tau have each two sounds associated with them. They are referred to Life, Peace, Wisdom, Riches, Grace, Fertility and Power. The two sounds of each letter are the hard and the soft — the aspirated and the softened. They are called Double, because each letter presents a contrast or permutation; thus Life and Death; Peace and War (Evil); Wisdom and Folly; Riches and Poverty; Grace and Indignation; Fertility and Solitude (Desolation); Power and Servitude.

2. These Seven Double Letters point out seven localities; Above, Below, East, West, North, South, and the Palace of Holiness in the midst of them sustaining all things.

3. These Seven Double Letters He designed, produced, and combined, and formed with them the Planets (stars) of this Universe, the Days of the Week, and the Gates of the soul (the orifices of perception) in Man. From these Seven He hath produced the Seven Heavens, the Seven Earths, the Seven Sabbaths : for this cause He has loved and blessed the number Seven, more than all things under Heaven (His Throne).

4. Two Letters produce two houses; three form six; four form twenty-four; five form one hundred and twenty; six form seven hundred and twenty;[39] seven form five thousand and forty; and beyond this their numbers increase so that the mouth can hardly utter them, nor the ear hear the number of them. So now, behold the Stars of the Universe (Planets) are Seven; the Sun, Venus, Mercury, Moon, Saturn, Jupiter and Mars. The Seven are also the Seven Days of Creation; and the Seven Gateways of the Soul of Man—the two eyes, the two ears, the mouth and the two nostrils. So with the Seven are formed the seven heavens,[41] the seven earths, and the seven periods of time; and so has He preferred the number Seven above all things under Heaven[42].

SUPPLEMENT TO CHAPTER IV

NOTE.—This is a modern illustration of the allotment of the Seven Letters; it is not found in the ancient copies of the "Sepher Yetzirah."

He produced Beth, and referred it to Wisdom; He crowned it, combined and formed with it the Moon in the Universe, the first day of the week, and the right eye of man.

He produced Gimel, and referred it to Health; He crowned it, combined and joined with it Mars in the Universe, the second day of the week, and the right ear of man.

He produced Daleth, and referred it to Fertility; He crowned it, combined and formed with it the Sun in the Universe, the third day of the week, and the right nostril of man.

He produced Kaph, and referred it to Life; He crowned it, combined and formed with it Venus in the Universe, the fourth day of the week, and the left eye of man.

He produced Pé, and referred it to Power; He crowned it, combined and formed with it Mercury in the Universe, the fifth day of the week, and the left ear of man.

He produced Resh, and referred it to Peace; He crowned it, combined and formed with it Saturn in the Universe, the sixth day of the week, and the left nostril of man.

He produced Tau, and referred it to Beauty; He crowned it, combined and formed with it Jupiter in the Universe, the Seventh Day of the week, and the mouth of man.

By these Seven letters were also made seven worlds, seven heavens, seven earths, seven seas, seven rivers, seven deserts, seven days, seven weeks from Passover to Pentecost, and every seventh year a Jubilee.

CHAPTER V

SECTION I. The Twelve Simple Letters are Heh, Vau, Zain, Cheth, Teth, Yod, Lamed, Nun, Samech, Oin, Tzaddi and Qoph[43]: they are the foundations of these twelve properties: Sight, Hearing, Smell, Speech, Taste, Sexual Love, Work, Movement, Anger, Mirth, Imagination[44] and Sleep. These Twelve are also allotted to the directions in space: North-east, South-east, the East above, the East below, the North above, the North below, the South-west, the North-west, the West above, the West below, the South above, and the South below; these diverge to infinity, and are as the arms of the Universe.

2. These Twelve Simple Letters he designed, and combined, and formed with them the Twelve celestial constellations of the Zodiac, whose signs are Teth, Shin, Tau, Samech, Aleph, Beth, Mem, Oin, Qoph, Gimel, Daleth and Daleth.[45] The Twelve are also the Months of the Year: Nisan[46] Yiar, Sivan, Tamuz, Ab, Elul, Tishri, Hesvan, Kislev, Tebet, Sabat and Adar. The Twelve are also the Twelve organs of living creatures,[47] the two hands, the two feet, the two kidneys, the spleen, the liver, the gall, private parts, stomach and intestines.

He made these, as it were provinces, and arranged them as in order of battle for warfare. And also the Elohim[48] made one from the region of the other.

Three Mothers and Three Fathers; and thence issue Fire, Air, and Water. Three Mothers, Seven Doubles and Twelve Simples.

3. Behold now these are the Twenty and Two Letters from which Jah, Jehovah Tzabaoth, the Elohim of the living, the God of Israel, exalted and sublime, the Dweller in eternity, formed and established all things; High and Holy is His Name.

SUPPLEMENT TO CHAPTER V

NOTE.—This is a modern illustration of the allotment of the Twelve Letters; it is not found in the ancient copies of the "Sepher Yetzirah."

----

1. God produced Hé, predominant in Speech, crowned it, combined and formed with it Aries in the Universe, Nisan in the Year, and the right foot of Man.

2. He produced Vau, predominant in mind, crowned it, combined and formed with it Taurus in the Universe, Aiar in the Year, and the right kidney of Man.

3. He produced Zain, predominant in Movement, crowned it, combined and formed it with Gemini in the Universe, Sivan in the Year, and the left foot of Man.

4. He produced Cheth, predominant in Sight, crowned it, combined and formed with it Cancer in the Universe, Tamuz in the Year, and the right hand of Man.

5. He produced Teth, predominant in Hearing, crowned it, combined and formed with it Leo in the Universe, Ab in the Year, and the left Kidney in Man.

6. He produced Yod, predominant in Work, crowned it, combined and formed with it Virgo in the Universe, Elul in the Year, and the left hand of Man.

7. He produced Lamed, predominant in Sexual desire, crowned it, combined and formed with it Libra in the Universe, Tishri in the Year, and the private parts of Man. (Kalisch gives "gall.")

8. He produced Nun, predominant in Smell, crowned it, combined and formed with it Scorpio in the Universe, Heshvan in the Year, and the intestines of Man.

9. He produced Samech, predominant in Sleep, crowned it, combined and formed with it Sagittarius in the Universe, Kislev in the Year, and the stomach of Man.

10. He produced Oin, predominant in Anger, crowned it, combined and formed with it Capricornus in the Universe, Tebet in the Year, and the liver of Man.

11. He produced Tzaddi, predominant in Taste, crowned it, combined and formed with it Aquarius in the Year, and the gullet in Man.

12. He produced Qoph, predominant in Mirth, crowned it, combined and formed with it Pisces in the Universe, Adar in the Year, and the spleen of Man.

CHATER VI

SECTION I. Three Fathers and their generations, Seven conquerors and their armies, and Twelve bounds of the Universe. See now, of these words, the faithful witnesses are the Universe, the Year and Man. The dodecad, the heptad, and the triad with their provinces; above is the Celestial Dragon, T L I,[49] and below is the World, and lastly the heart of Man. The Three are Water, Air and Fire; Fire above, Water below, and Air conciliating between them; and the sign of these things is that the Fire sustains (volatilizes) the waters; Mem is mute. Shin is sibilant, and Aleph is the Mediator and as it were a friend placed between them.

2. The Celestial Dragon, T L I, is placed over the universe like a king upon the throne; the revolution of the year is as a king over his dominion; the heart of man is as a king in warfare. Moreover, He made all things one from the other; and the Elohim set good over against evil, and made good things from good, and evil things from evil: with the good tested He the evil, and with the evil did He try the good. Happiness[50] is reserved for the good, and misery[51] is kept for the wicked.

3. The Three are One, and that One stands above. The Seven are divided; three are over against three, and one stands between the triads. The Twelve stand as in warfare; three are friends, three are enemies; three are life givers; three are destroyers. The three friends are the heart, the ears, and the mouth; the three enemies are the liver, the gall, and the tongue[52]; while God[53] the faithful king rules over all. One above Three, Three above Seven, and Seven above Twelve; and all are connected the one with the other.

4. And after that our father Abraham had perceived, and understood, and had taken down and engraved all these things, the Lord most high[55] revealed Himself, and called him His beloved, and made a Covenant with him and his seed; and Abraham believed on Him[56] and it was imputed unto him for righteousness. And He made this Covenant between the ten toes of the feet—this is like that of circumcision; and between the ten fingers of the hands and this is like that of the tongne.[57] And He bound the twenty-two letters unto his speech[58] and showed him all the mysteries of them.[59] He drew them through the Waters; He burned them in the Fire; He vibrated them in the Air;

Seven in the highest heavens; and Twelve in the celestial constellations of the Zodiac.

The End of the "Booh of Formation."

THE THIRTY-TWO PATHS OF WISDOM
Translated from the Hebrew Text of Joannes Stephanns Rittangelius, 1642.

THE First Path is called the Admirable or the Hidden Intelligence (the Highest Crown): for it is the Light giving the power of comprehension of that First Principle which has no beginning; and it is the Primal Glory, for no created being can attain to its essence.

The Second Path is that of the Illuminating Intelligence: it is the Crown of Creation, the Splendour of the Unity, equalling it, and it is exalted above, every head, and named by the Kabalists the Second Glory.

The Third Path is the Sanctifying Intelligence, and is the basis of foundation of Primordial Wisdom, which is called the Former of Faith, and its roots, Amen; and it is the parent of Faith, from whose virtues doth Faith emanate.

The Fourth Path is named Measuring, Cohesive or Receptacular; and is so called because it contains all the holy powers, and from it emanate all the spiritual virtues with the most exalted essences: they emanate one from the other by the power of the primordial emanation. (The Highest Crown.)[1]

The Fifth Path is called the Radical Intelligence, because it is itself the essence equal to the Unity, uniting itself to the Binah,[2] or Intelligence which emanates from the Primordial depths of Wisdom or Chokmah.[3]

The Sixth Path is called the Intelligence of the Mediating Influence, because in it are multiplied the influxes of the emanations, for it causes that influence to flow into all the reservoirs of the Blessings, with which these themselves are united.

The Seventh Path is the Occult Intelligence, because it is the Refulgent Splendour of all the Intellectual virtues which are perceived by the eyes of intellect, and by the contemplation of faith.

The Eighth Path is called Absolute or Perfect, because it is the means of the primordial, which has no root by which it can cleave, nor rest, except in the hidden places of *Gedulah*,[4] Magnificence, which emanate from its own proper essence.

The Ninth Path is the Pure Intelligence, so called because it purifies the Numerations, it proves and corrects the designing of their representation, and disposes their unity with which they are combined without diminution or division.

The Tenth Path is the Resplendent Intelligence, because it is exalted above every head, and sits on the throne of *Binah*, (the Intelligence spoken of in the Third Path). It illuminates the splendour of all the lights, and causes a supply of influence to emanate from the Prince of countenances.[5]

The Eleventh Path is the Scintillating Intelligence, because it is the essence of that curtain which is placed close to the order of the disposition, and this is a special dignity given to it that it may be able to stand before the Face of the Cause of Causes.

The Twelfth Path is the Intelligence of Transparency because it is that species of Magnificence called *Chazchazit*,[6] which is named the place whence issues the vision of those seeing in apparitions. (That is the prophecies by seers in a vision.)

The Thirteenth Path is named the Uniting Intelligence, and is so-called because it is itself the Essence of Glory. It is the Consummation of the Truth of individual spiritual things.

The Fourteenth Path is the Illuminating Intelligence, and is so called because it is that *Chashmal*[7] which is the founder of the concealed and fundamental ideas of holiness and of their stages of preparation.

The Fifteenth Path is the Constituting Intelligence, so called because it constitutes the substance of creation in pure darkness, and men have spoken of these contemplations; it is that darkness spoken of in Scripture, Job xxxviii. 9, "and thick darkness a swaddling band for it."

The Sixteenth Path is the Triumphal or Eternal Intelligence, so called because it is the pleasure of the Glory, beyond which is no other Glory like to it, and it is called also the Paradise prepared for the Righteous.

The Seventeenth Path is the Disposing Intelligence, which provides Faith to the Righteous, and they are clothed with the Holy Spirit by it, and it is called the Foundation of Excellence in the state of higher things.

The Eighteenth Path is called the House of Influence (by the greatness of whose abundance the influx of good things upon created beings is increased), and from the midst of the investigation the arcana and hidden senses are drawn forth, which dwell in its shade and which cling to it, from the cause of all causes.

The Nineteenth Path is the Intelligence of all the activities of the spiritual beings, and is so called because of the affluence diffused by it from the most high blessing and most exalted sublime glory.

The Twentieth Path is the Intelligence of Will, and is so called because it is the means of preparation of all and each created being, and by this intelligence the existence of the Primordial Wisdom becomes known.

The Twenty-first Path is the Intelligence of Conciliation, and is so called because it receives the divine influence which flows into it from its benediction upon all and each existence.

The Twenty-second Path is the Faithful Intelligence and is so called because by it spiritual virtues are increased, and all dwellers on earth are nearly under its shadow.

The Twenty-third Path is the Stable Intelligence, and it is so called because it has the virtue of consistency among all numerations.

The Twenty-fourth Path is the Imaginative Intelligence, and it is so called because it gives a likeness to all the similitudes which are created in like manner similar to its harmonious elegancies.

The Twenty-fifth Path is the Intelligence of Probation, or is Tentative, and is so called because it is the primary temptation, by which the Creator trieth all righteous persons.

The Twenty-sixth Path is called the Renovating Intelligence, because the Holy God renews by it all the changing things which are renewed by the creation of the world.

The Twenty-seventh Path is the Exciting Intelligence, and it is so called because through it is consummated and perfected the nature of every existent being under the orb of the Sun, in perfection.

The Twenty-ninth Path is the Corporeal Intelligence, so-called because it forms every body which is formed beneath the whole set of worlds and the increment of them.

The Thirtieth Path is the Collecting Intelligence, and is so-called because Astrologers deduce from it the judgment of the Stars, and of the celestial signs, and the perfections of their science, according to the rules of their resolutions.

The Thirty-first Path is the Perpetual Intelligence; but why is it so-called? Because it regulates the motions of the Sun and Moon in their proper order, each in an orbit convenient for it,

The Thirty-second Path is the Administrative Intelligence, and it is so called because it directs and associates in all their operations the seven planets, even all of them in their own due courses.

NOTES
TO THE
"SEPHER YETZIRAH."

It is of considerable importance to a clear understanding of this Occult treatise that the whole work be read through before comment is made, so that the general idea of the several chapters may become in the mind one concrete whole. A separate consideration of the several parts should follow this general grasp of the subject, else much confusion may result.

This book may be considered to be an Allegorical Parallel between the Idealism of Numbers and Letters and the various parts of the Universe, and it sheds much light on many mystic forms and ceremonies yet extant, notably upon Freemasonry, the Tarot, and the later Kabalah, and is a great aid to the comprehension of the Astro-Theosophic schemes of the Rosicrucians. To obtain the full value of this Treatise, it should be studied hand in hand with Hermetic Rituals, the "Isiac Tablet", and with a complete set of the Tarot designs.

Note that the oldest MSS. copies of the "Sepher Yetzirah" have no vowel points: the latest editions have them. The system of points in writing Hebrew was not perfected until the seventh century, and even then was not in constant use. Ginsburg asserts that the system of vowel polluting was invented by a Rabbi Mocha in Palestine about A.D. 570, who designed it to assist his pupils. But Isaac Myer states that there are undoubted traces of pointing in Hebrew MSS. of the second century.

The words "Sepher Yetzirah" are written in Hebrew from right to left, SPR YTzYRH, Samech Peh Rash, Yod Tzaddi Yod Resh Heh; modes of transliteration vary with different authors. Yod is variously written in English letters as I, Y, or J, or sometimes Ie. Tzaddi is properly Tz; but some write Z only, which is misleading because the Hebrew has also a true Z, Zain.

CHAPTER I.

THE twelve sections of this chapter introduce this philosophic disquisition upon the Formation and Development of the Universe. Having specified the subdivision of the letters into three classes, the Triad, the Heptad, and the Dodecad, these are put aside for the time; and the Decad mainly considered as

specially associated with the idea of Number, and as obviously composed of the
Tetrad and the Hexad.

I. *Thirty-two.* This is the number of the Paths or Ways of Wisdom, which are added as a supplement. 32 is written in Hebrew by LB, Lamed and Beth, and these are the last and first letters of the Pentateuch. The number 32 is obtained thus—2 x 2 x 2 x 2 x 2 = 32, Laib, LB as a Hebrew word, means the Heart of Man.

Paths. The word here is NTIBUT, netibuth; NTIB, meant primarily a pathway, or foot-made track; but is here used symbolically in the same sense as the Christian uses the word, *way*—the way of life: other meanings are—stage, power, form, effect; and later, a doctrinal formula, in Kabalistic writings.

2. *Jah.* This divine name is found in Psalm lxviii. 4; it is translated into Greek as hmos, and into Latin as *dominus,* and commonly into the English word, *Lord*: it is really the first half of the word IHVH or Jehovah, or the Yahveh of modern scholars.

3. *Jehovah Tzabaoth.* This divine name is printed in English Bibles as Jehovah Sabaoth, or as "Lord of hosts" as in Psalm xxiv. 10. TzBA is an *army.*

4. *God of Israel*, Here the word God is ALHI, which in unpointed Hebrew might be God, or Gods, or My God.

5. *The Elohim of the Living,* The words are ALHIM ChIIM. Alhim, often written in English letters as Elohim, or by Godfrey Higgins as Aleim, seems to be a masculine plural of the feminine form Eloah, ALH, of the divine masculine name EL, AL; this is commonly translated God, and means strong, mighty, supreme. Chiim, is the plural of Chi—*living*, or *life*. ChIH is a *living animal,* and so is ChIVA. ChII is also *life.* Frey in his dictionary gives ChIIM as the plural word, *lives,* or vitæ. The true adjective for *living* is ChIA. Elohim Chiim, then, apart from Jewish or Christian preconception, is "the living Gods," or "the Gods of the lives, *i.e.,* living ones." Rittangelius gives Dii viventes, "The living Gods," both words in the plural. Pistorius omits both words. Postellus, the orthodox, gives Deus Vivus. The Elohim are the Seven Forces, proceeding from the One Divine, which control the "terra viventium," the manifested world of life.

6. *God.* In this case we have the simple form AL, EL.

7. *Sepharim.* SPRIM, the plural mascuUne of SPR, commonly translated *book* or *letter:* the meaning here is plainly "forms of expression."

8. *Numbers. Letters and Sounds*, The three Hebrew words here given are, in unpointed Hebrew, SPR, SPR and SIPUR. Some late editors to cover the difficulty of this passage, have given SPR, SPUR, SIPR, pointing them to read Separ, Seepur, Saypar.

The sense of the whole volume appears to need their translation as Numbers, Letters and Sounds. Pistorius gave "scriptis, numeratis, pronunciatis." Postellus gave "Numerans, numerus, numeratus," thus losing the contrasted meanings; and so did Rittangelius, who gave "Numero, numerante, numerate."

9. *The ineffable Sephiroth.* The words are SPIRUT BLIMH, Sephiruth Belimah. The simplest translation is "the voices from nothing." The Ten Sephiruth of the Kabalah are the "Ten Primary Emanations from the Divine Source" which are the primal forces leading to all manifestation upon every plane in succession. Buxtorf gives for Sephiruth—predicationes logicæ. The word seems to me clearly allied to the Latin spiritus,— spirit, soul, wind; and is used by Quintilian as a sound, or noise. The meaning of *Belimah* is more doubtful. Rittangelius always gives "præter illud ineffabile." Pistorius gives "præter ineffabile." Postellus evades the difficulty and simply puts the word Belimah into his Latin translation. In Frey's Dictionary BLIMH is translated as *nothing,* without any other suggestion; BLI is "not", MH is "anything." In Kabalistic writings the Sephiruth, the Divine Voices and Powers, are called "ineffbilis," not to be spoken of, from their sacred nature.

10. The classification of the Hebrew letters into a Triad, Heptad and Dodekad, runs through the whole philosophy of the Kabalah. Many ancient authors added intentional blinds, such as forming the Triad of A.M.T., Ameth, truth; and of AMN, Amen.

11. The Two Covenants, by the Word or Spirit, and by the Flesh, made by Jehovah with Abraham, Genesis XVII. The Covenant of Circumcision was to be an outward and visible sign of the Divine promise made to Abraham and his offspring. The Hebrew word for circumcision is Mulah, MULH: note that MLH is also synonymous with DBR, dabar,—verbum or word.

12. Rittangelius gives "replace the formative power upon his throne." Postellus gives "restore the device to its place,"

13. *Abyss;* the word is OUMQ for OMQ, a depth, vastness, or valley.

14. Hermetic rituals explain this Yetziratic attribution.

15. *The Lord the only God.* The words are ADUN IChID AL, or "Adonai (as commonly written) the only EL."

16. *Seat.* The word is MOUN, dwelling, habitation, or throne.

17. *Lightning flash.* In the early edition the words "like scintillating flame" are used: the Hebrew word is BRQ. Many Kabalists have shown how the Ten Sephiruth are symbolized by the zig-zag lightning flash.

18. *God;* the Divine name here is Jehovah.

19. The text gives only RTzUAV ShUB—"currendo et redeundo," but the commentators have generally considered this to be a quotation from Ezekiel i. 14, referred to H ChIVT, the living creatures, kerubic forms.

20. The Spirit of the Gods of the Living. RUCh ALHIM ChIIM.; or as R. gives it "spiritus Deorum Viventium." Orthodoxy would translate these words "The spirit of the living God."

21. AL ChI H OULMIM; "the Living God of Ages," here the word God really is in the singular.

22. The Voice, Spirit and Word are QUL, RUCh. DBR. A very notable Hebrew expression of Divinatory intuition was BATh QUL, the Daughter of the Voice.

23. Formless and void. THU and BHU; these two words occur in Genesis i. 2, and are translated "waste and void."

24. Note the order in which the primordial elements were produced. First, Spirit (query Akasa, Ether) then Air, Vayu; then Water, Apas, which condenses into solid elementary Earth, Prithivi; and lastly from the Water He formed Fire.

25. The first name is often written Ophanim, the letters are AUPNIM, in the Vision of Ezekiel i. 16, the word occurs and is translated "Wheels." ShRPIM are the mysterious beings of Isaiah vi. 2; the word otherwise is translated *Serpent,* and in Numbers xxi. 6, as "fiery serpents": also in verse 8 as "fiery serpent" when Jehovah said "Make thee a fiery serpent and set it upon a pole." Kerubim. The Hebrew words are ChIVTh H QDSh, holy animals: I have ventured to put Kerubim, as the title of the other Biblical form of Holy mysterious animal, as given in I. Kings vi. 23 and Exodus xxv. 18, and indeed Genesis iii. 24. Bible dictionaries generally give the word as Cherubim, but in Hebrew the initial letter is always K and not Ch.

26. Three. In the first edition I overlooked this word *three;* and putting and for as, made four classes of serving beings.

27. This is verse 4 of Psalm civ.

28. Here follow the permutations of the name I H V, which is the Tetragrammaton—Jehovah, without the second or final Heh: IHV is a Tri-grammaton, and is more suitable to the third or Yetziratic plane. HVI is the imperative form of the verb *to be,* meaning *be thou;* HIV is the infinitive; and VIH is future. In IHV note that Yod corresponds to the Father; Heh to Binah, the Supernal Mother; and Vau to the Microprosopus—Son.

29. Note the subdivision of the Decad into the Tetrad—four elements; and the Hexad—six dimensions of space.

CHAPTER II.

THIS chapter consists of philosophic remarks on the twenty-two sounds and letters of the Hebrew alphabet, and hence connected with the air by speech, and it points out the uses of those letters to form words — the signs of ideas, and the symbols of material substances.

30. *Soul*; the word is NPSh, which is commonly translated soul, meaning the living personality of man, animal or existing thing: it corresponds almost to the Theosophic Prana *plus* the stimulus of Kama.

31. This is the modern classification of the letters into guttural, palatal, lingual, dental and labial sounds.

32. *The 231 Gates*. The number 242 is obtained by adding together all the numbers from 1 to 22. The Hebrew letters can be placed in pairs in 242 different positions; thus ab, ag, ad, up to at; then ba, bb, bg, bd, up to bt, and so on to ts, tt: this is in direct order only, without reversal; for the reason why eleven are deducted, and the number 231 specified, see the Table and Note 15 in the edition of Postellus.

33. *Non-existent*; the word is AIN, nothingness. Ain precedes Ain Suph, boundlessness; and Ain Suph Aur, Boundless Light.

34. *Body;* the word is GUP, usually applied to the animal material body, but here means "one whole."

CHAPTER III.

THIS chapter is especially concerned with the essence of the Triad, as represented by the Three Mothers, Aleph, Mem, and Shin. Their development in three directions is pointed out, namely in the Macrocosm or Universe; in the Year or in Time; and in the Microcosm or Man.

35. The importance of equilibrium is constantly reiterated in the Kabalah. The Siphra Dtzeniouta, or Book of Concealed Mystery, translated by MacGregor Mathers, in his "Kabalah Denudata," opens with a reference to this Equilibrium as a fundamental necessity of stable existence.

36. *Heavens*, The Hebrew word Heshamaim HShMIM, has in it the element of Aesh, fire, and Mim, water; and also Shem, name; *The* Name is IHVH, attributed to the elements. ShMA is in Chaldee a name for the Trinity (Parkhurst). ShMSh is the Sun, and Light, and a type of Christ, the Sun of Righteousness. Malachi iv. 2.

37. *Were produced;* the Hebrew word BRA, is the root. Three Hebrew words are used in the Bible to represent the idea of making, producing or creating.

BRIAH, Beriah, giving shape, Genesis i. I.

OShIH, Ashiah, completing. Genesis i. 31.

ITzIRH, Yetzirah, forming, Genesis ii. 7.

To these the Kabalists add the word ATzLH, with the meaning of "producing something manifest from the unmanifested."

38. These several formations then appear in a table thus:—

Emanation.	*Shin.*	*Aleph.*	*Mem.*
Macrocosm.	Primal Fire.	Spirit.	Primal Water.
Universe.	Heavens.	Atmosphere.	Water & Earth.
Man.	Terrestrial Fire.	Air.	The Earth.
Elements.	Head.	Chest.	Belly.
Year.	Heat.	Temperate.	Cold.

CHAPTER IV.

THIS is the special chapter of the Heptad, the powers and properties of the Seven. Here again we have the threefold attribution of the numbers and letters to the Universe, to the Year, and to Man. The supplemental paragraphs have been printed in modern form by Kalisch; they identify the several letters of the Heptad more definitely with the planets, days of the week, human attributes and organs of the senses.

39. These numbers have been a source of difference between the editors and copyists, hardly any two editors concurring. I have given the numbers arising from continual multiplication of the product by each succeeding unit from one to seven. 2x1=2, 2x3 = 6, 6x4 = 24, 24x5 = 120, 120x6 = 720, 720x7 = 5,040.

40. In associating the particular letters to each planet the learned Jesuit Kircher allots Beth to the Sun, Gimel to Venus, Daleth to Mercury, Kaph to Luna, Peh to Saturn, Resh to Jupiter, and Tau to Mars. Kalisch in the supplementary paragraphs gives a different attribution; both are wrong, as an adept cultured clairvoyant could prove. Consult the Tarot symbolism given by Court de Gebelin, Eliphaz Lévi, and my notes in the "Isiac Tablet of Bembo." The true attribution is however, not anywhere printed. The planet names here given are Chaldee words.

41. The Seven Heavens and the Seven Earths are printed with errors, and I believe intentional mistakes, in many occult ancient books. Private Hermetic MSS. have alone the correct names and spelling.

42. On the further attribution of these Seven letters, note that Postellus gives: Vita—Mors, Pax—afflictio, Sapientia—stultitia, Divitiæ (Opus)—paupertas, Gratia—opprobrium. Proles—sterilitas, Imperium—servitus. Pistorius gives: Vita—mors. Pax—bellum, Scientia—ignorantia, Divitiæ—paupertas. Gratia—abominatio, Semen (Proles)—sterilitas, Imperium (Dominatio)—servitus.

CHAPTER V.

THIS chapter is specially concerned with the Dodecad; the number twelve is itself pointed out, and the characters of its component units, once more in the three zones of the universe, year and man; the last paragraph gives a recapitulation of the whole number of letters: the Supplement gives a form of allotment of the several letters.

43. It is necessary to avoid confusion between these letters; different authors translate them in different manners. Heh or Hé,

H, must not be confused with Cheth, or Heth, Ch. Teth, Th also must be kept distinct from the final letter Tau, T, which is one of the double letters; the semi-English pronunciation of these two letters is much confused, each is at times both t and th; Yod is either I, Y, or J; Samech is simple S, and must not be confused with Shin, Sh, one of the mother letters; Oin is often written in English Hebrew grammars as Ayin, and sometimes as Gnain; Tzaddi must not be confused with Zain, Z; and lastly Qoph, Q is very often replaced by K, which is hardly defensible as there is a true K in addition.

44. Postellus gives *suspicion,* and Pistorius, *mind.*

45. These letters are the initials of the 12 Zodiacal signs in Hebrew nomenclature. They are:

Teth	Telah	Aries	Mem	Maznim	Libra
Shin	Shor	Taurus	Oin	Oqereb	Scorpio
Tau	Thaumim	Gemini	Qoph	Qesheth	Sagittarius
Samech	Sartan	Cancer	Gimel	Gedi	Capricornus
Aleph	Aryeh	Leo	Daleth	Dali	Aquarius
Beth	Bethuleh	Virgo	Daleth	Dagim	Pisces

46. The month Nisan begins about March .29th. Yiar is also written Iyar, and Aiar: the Hebrew letters are AIIR.

47. The list of organs varies. All agree in, two hands, two feet, two kidneys, liver, gall and spleen. Postellus then gives, "intestina, vesica, arteriæ", the intestines, bladder and arteries; Rittangelius gives the same. Pistorius gives, "colon, coagulum et ventriculus," colon—the large intestine, coagulum and stomach. The chief difficulty is with the Hebrew word MSS., which is allied to two different roots, one meaning *private, concealed, hidden*; and the other meaning *liquefied.*

48. The Elohim—divine powers—not IHVH the Tetragrammaton,

CHAPTER IV.

THIS chapter is a *resumé* of the preceding five; it calls the universe and mankind to witness to the truth of the scheme of distribution of the powers of the numbers among created forms, and concludes with the narration that this philosophy was revealed by the Divine to Abraham, who received and faithfully accepted it, as a form of Wisdom under a Covenant.

49. The Dragon, TLI, Theli. The Hebrew letters amount in numeration to 440, that is 400, 30 and 10. The best opinion is that Tali or Theli refers to the 12 Zodiacal constellations along the great circle of the Ecliptic; where it ends there it begins again, and so the ancient occultists drew the Dragon with its tail in it's mouth. Some have thought that Tali referred to the constellation Draco, which meanders across the Northern polar sky; others have referred it to the Milky Way; others to an imaginary line joining Caput to Cauda Draconis, the upper and lower nodes of the Moon. Adolphe Franck says that Theli is an Arabic word.

50. *Happiness*, or a *good end*, or simply *good*, TUBH.

51. *Misery*, or an *evil end*, or simply *evil*, ROH.

52. This Hebrew version omits the allotment of the remaining six. Mayer gives the paragraph thus:—The triad of amity is the heart and the two ears; the triad of enmity is the liver, gall, and the tongue;. the three life-givers are the two nostrils and the spleen; the three death-dealing ones are the mouth and the two lower openings of the body.

53. *God.* In this case the name is AL, El.

54. This last paragraph is generally considered to be less ancient than the remainder of the treatise, and by another author.

55. The Lord most high. OLIU ADUN. Adun or Adon, or Adonai, ADNI, are commonly translated *Lord;* Eliun, OLIUN, is the more usual form of "the most high one."

56. *Him.* Rittangelius gives "credidit in Tetragrammaton," but this word is not in the Hebrew.

57. *Tongue.* The verbal covenant.

58. *Speech.* The Hebrew has "upon his tongue."

59. The Hebrew version of Rabbi Judah Ha Levi concludes with the phrase, "and said of him. Before I formed thee in the belly, I knew thee." Rabbi Luria, gives the Hebrew version which I have translated. Postellus gives: "He drew him into the water. He rose up in spirit, He inflamed him in. seven suitable forms with twelve signs." Mayer gives: "Er zog sie mit Wasser, Zundet sie an mit Feuer; erregte sie mit Geist; verbannte sie mit sieben, goss sie aus mit den zwolf Gestimen." "He drew them with water. He kindled them with fire. He moved them with spirit, distributed them with seven, and sent them forth with twelve."

NOTES TO THE THIRTY-TWO PATHS.

1. The highest Crown is Kether, the First Sephira, the first emanation from the Ain Suph Aur, the Limitless Light.

2. Binah, is the Third Sephira.

3. Chokmah, is the Second Sephira.

4. Gedulah, is a synonym of Chesed, the Fourth Sephira.

5. Metatron.

6. This word is from ChZCh, a seer, seership. Chazuth, is a vision.

7. This word means "scintillating flame."

The Thirty-two Paths are the Ten Sephiruth and the Twenty-two letters, each supplying a type of divine power and attributes.

Made in the USA
Lexington, KY
24 April 2018